Summary of Elon Musk:

Tesla, SpaceX and the Quest for a Fantastic Future

By: Ashlee Vance

Proudly Brought to you by:

Legal & Disclaimer

Legal & Disclaimer

Table of Contents

The Book at a Glance

The reporter, *Ashlee Vance*, had long awaited to accomplish something that many writers and reporters failed to do: write a book on the life story of **Elon Musk**. The multimillionaire clearly stated that he will not cooperate in this project but Vance was not giving up. He gathered information from the former employees of Musk to get the book started. So, when the famous innovator and businessman, Elon Musk, called him for dinner one day, he took the opportunity to get him to cooperate.

Musk's life journey was **not a sweet ride**. The man experienced more suffering than what an average person could take. He graduated from college with a degree in business and physics. Since he was a child, he had been dreaming of creating things that will make the future of humanity a brighter one. After graduating from the University, he took a shot at his dream and went to *Silicon Valley* to get started. That's when he created *Zip2* with his brother. The company gave businesses the chance to be on the internet. Compaq Computer proceeded to purchase Zip2 and Musk became one of the dot-com multimillionaire of that decade.

Musk turned to the finance industry and decided that banks needed a major upgrade to serve more customers. That's when *X.com* came to life. The company was an online financial institution and soon enough, it underwent a merger. Later, this company became what you know of today as **PayPal**.

To tell the tale about Elon Musk properly, Vance decided to study **SpaceX** first, one of the leading companies in the **aeronautics industry**. The headquarters of the company was something straight out of a science fiction movie.

It was not long after that he went into the automotive industry with **Tesla Motors**, a company committed to creating cars that are fully powered by *electricity*. Musk had long been obsessed with the idea of **electric cars** so when a couple of young engineers showed him their progress into making one, he did not hesitate to fund their projects.

The journey to making this company grow was **not a sweet one**. These were companies made during the **recession**. Almost every business was experiencing a downfall and it was not surprising that both companies suffered great losses. Musk lost all his fortune and his marriage crumbled.

This, however, did not stop Musk from continuing his dreams. **The failures he experienced were more than what an average person could take.** Those experiences affected Musk's mental and physical state, but he continued to focus on his work. His level of interest in the things that he found amusing pushed him to go beyond his boundaries until he made a name for himself in the space business, automotive industry, and in the utility industry.

Now, the name **Elon Musk** is one of the most respected names in these industries which nobody thought would achieve such developments. It was all thanks to the child who grew up to take his fantasies seriously.

CHAPTER 1: ELON'S WORLD

Ashlee Vance was to meet Elon Musk at a seafood restaurant located in Silicon Valley for dinner. However, as expected, Musk was late. He arrived 15 minutes later wearing designer jeans. With Musk's built and height, one would think that he is one of those intimidating alpha males in the society. However, this person was much more sheepish. It took minutes before he was able to warm up and be at ease.

That dinner's purpose was for Vance and Musk to **negotiate** on certain terms regarding a book. **Eighteen months ago**, Ashlee Vance planned to write a book about the life of Elon Musk. However, the latter did not approve of the idea. Musk stated that he would not cooperate with Vance in making this book. However, this did not stop the reporter from continuing with his idea. He had other means of getting the information he needed.

Vance proceeded to ask the former employees of Musk who had worked in Tesla Motors and SpaceX. He also did not hesitate to ask some of Musk's friends for help. Days after days and months after months, Vance asked an estimated number of **200 people** about *Elon Musk*.

Subsequently, the reporter received a call from Musk. The businessman told him that he could make this project a difficult one for Vance or he could cooperate and help him. Fortunately for the reporter, Musk chose the latter. He was willing to cooperate. Of course, there were conditions for Musk to help. He wants to read the book before it was published. He was also planning to add footnotes to the book. Musk wants to set the record straight and avoid any inaccurate and unnecessary information to be placed in a book that anybody can read.

One of the things that one should know about Musk is that he is **tormented** every time he sees any inaccuracies in facts. He also tends to answer simple questions with a **wordy explanation**. Vance understands his perspective. **Musk wants a certain control over his story.** However, Vance did not accept these conditions. He cannot let Musk read the book before its publication for professional, personal, and practical reasons. The reporter understood that Musk has his own version of the truth. However, this version of the truth may not be the same as the truth of the other people around him.

The two started discussing the people involved in **public relations**. Nevertheless, the conversation quickly came to their **mutual acquaintances**, *Howard Hughes*, and the *Tesla factory*. In the middle of their discussions, they ordered something to eat. Musk asked for a low-carb diet on the menu and the two continued. The businessman told Vance about the biggest fear he had.

Musk said that he is afraid of ***Larry Page***, the <u>co-founder and CEO of Google</u>, making an army of **artificial intelligence-enhanced robots** that may lead to the **destruction of humanity**. This is rather surprising since Musk and Page are close friends. He considers Page as a kind-natured individual and he is, in no way, an evil scientist plotting mankind's end. However, things do not go as planned all the time. Musk strongly believes that something could go wrong along the way and he might create something evil along the way.

It was not long when Musk asked the reporter why he wanted to write a book about him. He wanted to know Vance's intentions in this project. It took the reporter forty-five minutes to discuss his reasons behind this idea, and how Musk should let him write a book without his control on certain parts.

Another thing to remember about Elon Musk is his appreciation for people with **resolution**. He respects people who are determined in what they are doing. There were already a couple of writers and reporters who wanted to delve deeper into the life of Elon Musk but it was **only** Ashlee Vance who kept on pursuing this idea despite all the rejections from Musk.

At the end of their discussions, Musk granted Vance access to the CEOs of his companies, his family, and his friends. For the <u>first time</u>, a reporter is finally telling the story of ***Elon Musk***. The dinner ended with the prominent businessman and innovator asking this question: **"Do you think I'm insane?"** However, it was more like a question meant for himself than for the reporter.

Vance proceeded with his investigation on Musk's life. He believes that any study about him should start with **SpaceX**. This company is the embodiment of Musk's stated **<u>life purpose</u>**. Elon Musk dreams of a bright future for humankind where men can finally be multi-planetary species. He dreams for humans to be **<u>space colonizers</u>**.

His ideas sound absurd but nonetheless, Musk's attitude of attempting impossible things is the reason that a lot of people respect him. However, it would seem that his computers designed to save the world are not performing well.

In the **early 2012**, the world was able to witness innovations of Musk's companies that helped open a new era in the industry. ***SpaceX*** was able to launch a capsule for the **International Space Station** and this capsule landed on Earth safely. Tesla Motors also released the Model S, a vehicle solely run by <u>electricity</u>.

Musk is also the chairman and the largest shareholder of a solar energy company that is making a name for itself, SolarCity.

This success, however, is not something that came on Musk's first try. The money he got from selling his first company, ***Zip2***, was used to build <u>SpaceX</u>, <u>Tesla Motors</u>, and <u>SolarCity</u>. He founded these companies during the <u>downfall</u> of many companies in the industry. It was not long when Musk's fortune was gone.

This failure did not stop him and now, he is probably one of the most prominent person in the space business, automotive industry, and in the utility industry.

CHAPTER 2: AFRICA

It was in **1984** that Elon Musk was introduced to the public. The PC and Office Technology publication of South Africa that focuses on trade featured the game that Musk created. It is a sci-fi game where the player needs to defeat an alien space freighter.

But it was way before this time that Musk started envisioning and working on his dreams. A child imagining battles between the forces of good and evil is amazing and adorable but for a child to take these battles seriously, that is one remarkable act. Elon belongs to the latter. His mind perfectly blended **fantasy** and **reality** to the point where the two were **inseparable**. Humanity's destiny became an obligation for him.

Musk's role-model and inspiration was his **grandfather**, Joshua Norman Haldeman. Haldeman was an athletic person who was into horseback riding, wrestling, and boxing. Haldeman was an adventurous person. He was a pilot and an author. He wrote a book with his wife about being a poor private pilot. Their family lived in a house with a dance studio.

The *Haldeman's* had everything they needed but the family gave up the life that they had to start an adventure. With their **single-engine plane**, they flew to **Africa**, **Scotland**, and **Norway**. They even went to *Australia*. They became famous for being the first ones to fly from Africa to Australia with the use of a single-engine plane. The Haldeman's also embarked on a journey to look for the **Lost City of the Kalahari Desert** in *Africa*.

Musk's grandparents raised their children using the **Laissez-faire approach**. They instilled into the minds of their children that they can do anything that they want because they are capable of doing what they dream of. This kind of upbringing was carried down to Musk's generation.

Errol Musk and Maye Haldeman, Musk's parents, were childhood friends. His father was part of the cool kids while his mother was considered a nerd. It took seven years for Errol to court Maye. They have three children with Elon Musk being the oldest. Errol was a mechanical and electrical engineer who worked on the construction of office buildings, subdivisions, and an air force base. Maye, on the other hand, was a dietician.

Elon Musk was curious and energetic since young. However, despite this, he had learned to build a wall between his world and the world outside his mind. When people spoke to him, he did not respond, which led to his parents thinking that he was *deaf*. The doctor suggested him to take adenoid glands for him to hear more clearly. However, nothing changed after the operation. The young Elon continued thinking on his own while being considered **rude** or **weird**.

When he was just five or six years old, he shut out the world from his mind. This was a pleasant experience for him. He was able to think and **concentrate** without any interruptions. His dedication to completing a single task is commendable.

His mind can see images in great details like how computers now can show you the layout used by engineers. The young boy was also a **compulsive reader**. He is always reading or holding a book. Musk spent **ten hours** of his day reading.

At the age of **14**, Elon Musk experienced an *existential crisis*. He turned to **religious texts** and **philosophical theories**, but in the end, he went back to the sci-fi books he loved as a child. *Douglas Adams' The Hitchhiker's Guide* *to the Galaxy* became one of the books that had the most influence on Musk. He stated that finding the answers to questions are easy. **It is finding the questions to ask that makes the process complicated.** The teenage Musk came up with the conclusion that all we can do is to strive for a greater *collective enlightenment.*

The Afrikaner culture that Musk grew up with made a huge impact on his personality. Hyper masculine behavior was given more tolerance and respect. This is the exact behavior of Musk. His geeky attitude did not fit in. There were many times when he planned to go away and be in a place where he can turn his dreams into reality. He was one of the people who saw *America* as the land of opportunities.

He was able to go to America after there was an amendment to the law that allowed his mother to transfer her citizenship to her children. It took a year to prepare all the needed papers and another three weeks to get a **plane ticket**. Then he left.

CHAPTER 3: CANADA

Musk's transfer to **Canada** was not properly planned. He was supposed to stay in his uncle's house. However, a letter came to Maye Musk while Elon was on his way to Canada. His uncle was in Minnesota at that time. Musk had nowhere to stay so he went to a youth hostel. Later on, he bought a countrywide bus ticket for $100 to look for his mother's other relatives in Canada. Finally, Musk managed to stay in the house of his cousin.

Life in Canada was far from what he expected. Musk had to do **various odd jobs** to support himself. He tried **tending vegetables** and **shoveling grain bins** in his cousin's farm. But the hardest job came when he inquired at the unemployment office. Musk asked for the highest paid job and got himself a work as a <u>cleaner</u> of a boiler room in a lumber mill. He earned $18 every hour.

Kimbal, Musk's brother, went to Canada and the two reunited. After some time, Musk enrolled in **Queen's University** in *Ontario*. Both of them would spend time reading the newspaper and finding interesting people. They would then call them and ask if they want to have lunch.

One of these people was Peter Nicholson, an executive in a bank. Nicholson found the call interesting and arranged for the three of them to have lunch together. However, it took six months before they met. He was quite impressed with how the two acted. Kimbal was a charming lad while Elon was a more reserved one.

Musk met *Justine Wilson*, his former wife, during his time in the university. Wilson felt that both of them were always competing. Their relationship was on and off. The two dated other people but in the end, Musk keeps on going back to Wilson. He was so persistent until he was able to win her over.

He was placed in the international section of the dorm where Canadian students are paired with international students. Musk attended the **least number of classes** as he could. He would spend his time **selling computer parts** and **PCs**. He would also make something for the other students like a word processor for a cheaper fee. Students with broken computers would go to him for help.

College gave Musk more opportunities to hone his skills. He was more ambitious than he was in high school. He joined **public-speaking contests** and **studied businesses courses**.

Navaid Farooq, his dormmate in the international section, described Musk as a different person in terms of his attitude when he gets into something. He has a different level of interest compared to most people.

After two years, Musk transferred to the *University of Pennsylvania* with a **scholarship**. His field of interest broadened as he studied economics and physics. There, he met many people like him. Because of this, Musk felt more comfortable in school. He continued his relationship with Justine Wilson and sometimes, they would visit each other and spend time together.

<u>Solar power</u> had long been a subject of Musk's interest and this pushed him to make a paper about it. His professor found his work excellent.

He began planning about what he would do after college. It crossed his mind to enter the **video game business** since he's an avid fan. But as he gave it more thought, Musk came to a conclusion that this is not the career that he should pursue.

Wealth was not Musk's driving force to succeed in his endeavors. He has always been following his own personal plan. He believes that making technologies that will both be important and useful in the future is the path that he should take.

CHAPTER 4: ELON'S FIRST START-UP

It was in **1994** when *Elon* and *Kimbal Musk* decided to take a trip around the country. Kimbal worked as a franchisee for **College Pro Painters**. This resulted in a small business. But to start their journey to being full-fledged Americans, he sold his part of the franchise. The money he got was added to what Elon has. Together they bought a used BMW.

Then they started their road trip. Their first stop was **San Francisco**. It was a rough journey for the two. They had to deal with the changes of the weather condition in the area. Despite that, this journey gave them plenty of time to think and daydream.

From San Francisco, they traveled to Colorado, Wyoming, South Dakota, and Illinois. It must be in their blood to have the urge to travel and embark on an adventure.

Eventually, they had to go back to enroll Elon in the university. Their adventure resulted to an idea of creating an **online network** that <u>doctors</u> can use. Its purpose is for doctors to exchange information and work together. They made the necessary preparations but the idea was not pushed through due to the lack of interest.

Musk went to Silicon Valley during the summer. He had to handle <u>two internships every day</u>. During the day, he had to work at the *Pinnacle Research Institute*. They were researching about ultracapacitors and it could be used for electric and hybrid vehicles. At night, he had to work at the *Rocket Science Games*. They find ways on how to improve video games.

Some of the people working in the group are responsible for the success of some Apple products. There are even people who had worked on the very first **Star Wars**. Individuals who worked for the Lucas Arts Entertainment were also present. Musk was given the task of making *basic level codes*. To be specific, he was tasked to write drivers that will let joysticks and mice communicate with the computers. *Silicon Valley* became the place where Musk found an opportunity to make his dream a reality.

An idea struck him during his days as an intern. Musk wanted to make a company that will let businesses be on the internet. This is something that nobody had ever attempted before. This idea is what gave birth to *Zip2*.

It was a tough start for Musk. Despite the brilliant idea he had, nobody believed that it was necessary. He asked Kimbal for help and the both of them went to work. They had to convince businesses to accept their idea. Because of Kimbal's personality, he was assigned to the sales operations. He advertised their product to different businesses. Musk was assigned to the coding.

They rented a place for their small company. A **faster internet connection** was needed so they had a deal with the internet service provider in the same building where their office is located. They acquired the technology used by *Navteq* for digital maps for free. Musk was able to have the database for the business listings at a cheap price. He combined these databases to come up with their system.

The two brothers were broke for the first few months of their operations. All their money was invested in their company. Their father gave them **$28000** to fund their business. Due to financial constraints, they had to live in the office.

The majority did not openly accept the idea of their system. It was not working all the time and no one was really buying for the **first few months**. However, the continuous improvements they were having provided Elon, Kimbal, and their employees with enough **motivation** to continue.

They kept going and finally attained success. The company was making a name for itself. Zip2 was constantly featured in published materials. Eventually, a merger was planned with *CitySearch*. But Zip2 was not fully committed to the idea. There were oppositions and the merger was cancelled. Musk lost his position as the chairman and the company suffered a great loss.

Zip2 was losing more and more money. However, Compaq Computer suddenly offered to purchase the company. With its current condition, the board did not hesitate to take up the offer. Elon received **$22 million** while Kimbal had **$15 million**.

Musk reflected on his actions when he was still in Zip2. The way he handled his employees made them lose confidence in themselves. Being a leader was not his forte but he still strived to be one.

CHAPTER 5: PAYPAL MAFIA BOSS

With Musk's realization from his previous experiences in Zip2 when it came to his coworkers and employees, one would probably think that he learned his lesson. Unfortunately, history was about to repeat itself and this time, it's worse.

The sale of Zip2 made Musk more ambitious. He finally became a dot-com millionaire. He leveled up just like the players in the video games that he played as a child. This experience fired up his ambitious attitude. He looked for another industry that needed improvement.

Musk once worked as the head of strategy in a bank. He remembered the time when he found out how the bank can double its earnings through the **Brady bonds** issued by the U.S. government to help the third world countries with their *debts*. Unfortunately, the CEO of the bank rejected his plan. That gave Musk the idea that bankers may have the money but they are *dumb*.

The **finance industry** needed an *upgrade* and Musk could be a big influence in this change with just a small amount of investment. He discussed his plans with the **Pinnacle Research** but the group believed that the industry was not ready for such improvement. Musk wanted to make a **financial institution online** that offers the same services like that of the normal ones you see in cities. Checking accounts, savings, brokerage services, and insurance services will all be available on the online financial institution that Musk is planning.

This posed a high risk on the part of Musk and his future customers. If anything went wrong with the system and the finances of the customers were messed up, it would be a huge problem.

But Musk put his plan into action anyway. That idea gave way to the creation of **X.com**, and this happened even before Zip2 was sold. After receiving his share on the purchase of his previous company, Musk became a multimillionaire at the age of **27**. He could finally afford all the luxuries he wanted. **He bought a condo, a luxury car, and a prop plane**. After all, he was part of the dot-com millionaire. He even had **CNN** film the delivery of his car.

Ed Ho, one of the co-founders of X.com, described Musk as a man who takes huge risks. No matter how many people warned him about his plans and ideas, he always tried his best to make them a reality.

Together with three others, Musk was able to create X.com. They may have the same way of thinking when it comes to the banking industry but their personalities were different. Harris Fricker wanted the company to be conventional. But Musk had other ideas. He wanted to make **major changes** in the **banking industry**.

It was not long before the clash of their ideas became a bigger problem. Fricker started a **coup** against Musk **after five months** from the establishment of X.com. Most of the employees and executives left Musk and sided with Fricker. However, he did not seem to let that experience get the best of him.

Musk continued running the company despite the lack of financial and human resources. He looked for investors that can help him and hired more people. He was able to acquire a **banking license** and a

15

mutual fund license. Musk operated the company using the essential banking concepts. He wanted to make a financial institution that provides **faster banking transactions**.

The presence of competitors was inevitable. A pair of teenagers made a company called **Confinity** that was later renamed to be *PayPal*. The relationship between the two companies was good but it did not last long. The two companies later had an intense battle on providing better services to their customers. The rivalry between the two led to a financial problem on both sides. This resulted in a merger.

However, this merger did not stop the two sides from heated debates on what idea was better. Soon after, Musk was left to manage an injured company. But something worse was about to come. Another coup against Musk was started. This became one of the worst coups in Silicon Valley. **The influence that Musk had on the company was fading and X.com became PayPal.**

It took quite some time for the situation to go back to normal and finally Musk was able to take a vacation with his wife. The vacation did not end well due to the **disease** he got while in Africa. Musk was diagnosed with the **strongest type of malaria**. He underwent a <u>near death experience</u> and he spent six months to recover. After that, Musk reached a conclusion that vacations will kill you.

CHAPTER 6: MICE IN SPACE

On the same year that X.com was renamed to PayPal, Elon Musk turned **30** years old. A realization hit him; he was no longer a "**child prodigy**". Life in Silicon Valley was way worse during Musk's time as compared to today. Wilson believed that people never really understood the sacrifices Musk had in order to reach the position that he has today.

Musk and Wilson decided that it was time for a change. The couple moved to Los Angeles to start a family. There was something in Los Angeles, as Wilson claimed, that suits Musk.

After the incident with PayPal, Musk left the internet industry and went back to his fantasies as a child which were rocket ships and space travels. With *Los Angeles* being the **haven of the aeronautics industry**, Musk saw the light in achieving his childhood dreams.

Los Angeles is the home of companies belonging to the space industry; in fact, most of the company's experimentation and manufacturing are mostly done in the area. Many people had the same ideas as Musk. Then he found the Mars Society, a nonprofit group with a purpose of exploring Mars. They even had the dream dream of settling on the planet.

The group was having a fundraiser to finance their projects when *Robert Zubrin*, the head of Mars Society, received a check of **$5000** from Musk. Nobody from the group knew him. Zubrin proceeded to inform Musk of the group's plans and experiments. He even invited him to the group's event. Musk sat with James Cameron, famous movie director and space enthusiast, and Carol Stoker, a planetary scientist working in NASA. The dinner was mainly about Cameron persuading Musk to fund his new movie and Zubrin convincing him to donate to Mars Society.

Musk made a **huge donation** to the group to fund their project. That time, Mars Society was planning to send mice to Mars. However, it was not only limited to sending mice to Mars. Part of the plan was to bring the mice back to Earth and have them procreate during the journey. It was an absurd idea for some. Most might not even consider funding it. Musk, however, did not care about the opinions and jokes of other people. **Space exploration is an important matter for him**. He believes that this holds the future for humanity. Mankind needs to go beyond their boundaries and that is what Musk is doing.

The idea of entering the space business finally became a reality for Musk. After a lot of arrangements, misunderstandings, and fights with many people, the **Space Exploration Technologies** was finally established. This was America's shot in this industry. Musk became more and more ambitious. The beginnings of SpaceX were rough, but after all the hard work they put into their project, they were able to launch their very first rocket. The first attempt, however, was a failure. The rocket crashed and an unnamed technician was blamed for the incident. The technician was dismayed and enraged to hear that his team was blamed for the crash. He exchanged a heated debate with Musk. It was later found out that the part that caused the crash was **rusted**.

A year later, the company took another chance and **launched another rocket**. With all the hard work and sacrifices of the team, they thought that this would be a successful one. They were thorough in correcting the mistakes that lead to the crash of their first attempt. Unfortunately, this second attempt also resulted in failure. This costly mistake took a toll on the engineers of SpaceX, but Musk remained to be *optimistic*.

All the failures he experienced never made Musk doubt his abilities. It didn't stop him from continuing. One of the things about Musk that Pete Worden, a former air force general, found impressive was how this man thinks. **He thinks big**.

CHAPTER 7: ALL ELECTRIC

Musk did not settle on conquering the *aeronautics industry*. He started entering the **automotive** business. A dinner with ***Harold Rosen*** and ***JB Straubel*** marked the beginning of Musk's journey to the automotive world.

Straubel was a Stanford graduate and pilot who wants to fly. He was passionate about creating electric vehicles and lessening the impact of gasoline to the planet. However, there were not many people who were as enthusiastic as Straubel in the idea. Except for one person. Straubel shared with Musk his idea of making **electric planes** but the latter was not interested in the idea of electric powered planes. But when Straubel mentioned about *electronic cars*, Musk was all ears. They later became friends and Musk funded the project of Straubel.

But it was not only them who had the idea of making a car powered by **lithium-ion battery**. Martin Eberhard and Mark Tarpenning started *NuvoMedia*, a company responsible for electronic book readers. **Gemstar International Group** took an interest in their company and bought it for $187 million. The two then thought of other things that they can do. That's when they started **Tesla Motors**, an automotive company that pledged to make electric cars.

Thinking of venturing into the automotive industry is one thing, but actually putting the plan in action is a whole different story. Making cars promised a challenging journey for the two, but after doing their research, they found out that the things that they need to worry about are the internal combustion research, advertising their products, and the final assembly of the parts. They can get the other parts of the car from different manufacturers.

Elon Musk became one of the prospective investors for the Tesla Motors. Eberhard and Tarpenning proceeded to discuss their projects with Musk and received a **$6.5 million investment**. This made Musk the largest shareholder of Tesla Motors.

When Eberhard and Tarpenning found out the battery that they needed for their cars, they went to work. Tesla grew and accommodated more engineers. By **2004**, they were able to create a new car with the help of **18 people**. Seeing this success, Musk invested more money into the company. After a few months, a second car was made.

However, the engineers found out that the combustion of batteries was more dangerous than the combustion of gasoline. Instead of providing a safer vehicle to people, they were actually making a more dangerous one. Six people were assigned to work on this problem. They were able to solve the issue. By **2006**, Tesla Motors decided to show the world their product.

They had a display in an event where *Arnold Schwarzenegger* and *Michael Eisner* showed up to have a test ride on the new car. By the end of the event, **30** people promised to purchase a car including Brin and Page, the co-founders of Google. Musk announced that they are to release a new model that will cost less.

But things didn't go as planned. One of the biggest mistakes of the company's executives lies in the transmission systems used in the Roadster. They worked on finding a solution to their problem but none of those probable solutions solved the issue. They were not able to deliver the cars in November 2007 due to this problem.

Another failure that the company committed was **underestimating** the **expenses** of manufacturing the new model. The cost of making a car tremendously exceeded its target selling price. It was a difficult moment for the company and its employees. Eberhard, the CEO of Tesla, knew that he had to do something to motivate his people. He lifted the morale of the employees by reminding them that they are not making cars for the money. They are doing this to change the people's perspective on what a car is.

Later on, Musk replaced Eberhard as the **CEO** of the company. He was demoted, and after some time, he left the company. Tesla did not actually mind losing most of the employees that they had from the beginning. Because of this, they could hire more talented individuals to work in the company.

However, recession came and the company no longer had the same problems in engineering and marketing. They are now facing a **huge financial problem** as their funds started to vanish. No one was buying cars and most companies were getting bankrupt. Because of this, Musk lost his money and he almost suffered a **nervous breakdown**.

CHAPTER 8: PAIN, SUFFERING AND SURVIVAL

Robert Downey, Jr had always admired Howard Hughes. Looking at the set of the Iron Man movie made him felt nostalgic. The set was once part of the Hughes Aircraft. This place was once a witness to how a man took a lot of industries by surprise through his ideals.

He heard about a man who had the same personality as Hughes. Elon Musk was a man who did things the way that he wanted to, and Downey had the urge to pay this person a visit. He went to SpaceX, which was just ten miles away from where they were filming the first Iron Man movie.

Downey was surprised to see SpaceX, and Musk gave him a tour of the facility personally. There were a lot of people working and machines being operated. He found similarities in Musk's company and the setting of the Iron Man film. Downey thought of Musk as an **unpretentious** person. The actor once again found similarities, but this time it was between **Elon Musk** and **Tony Stark**, his role in the movie. Both were dedicated to their work.

When he returned to the set, Downey told the director to put a *Tesla Roadster* inside Tony Stark's workshop. It was placed near the desk of Stark to symbolize the bond that Downey, Stark, and Musk had.

Jon Favreau later talked about how Elon Musk inspired *Robert Downey Jr* in his portrayal of Marvel's Tony Stark. It was not that long ago when Musk himself attended parties in Hollywood. He became friends with famous celebrities and prominent people in the entertainment industry. Justine Wilson made sure to properly document every party and happening in their lives on her blog. Her blog entries were composed of their moments with their well-known friends.

The press was interested in the life of Musk and how he spent time with his friends. He was able to keep up a good face despite the downfalls that his company was experiencing. The conditions of **SpaceX** and **Tesla** were definitely _not good_ and things started to change. Tesla had to start from the beginning after their failures and SpaceX still had employees in *Kwajalein* after their crashed rockets. Nevertheless, despite those problems, Musk was able to stay calm. His employees did not panic and he did his best to take care of them.

However, Musk's businesses were not the only things that suffered. Because of the constant problems in work, Musk and Wilson's marriage started to crumble. Wilson felt like a trophy wife and Musk did not tell her the real situation of the companies. He filed for divorce without informing Wilson. Eventually, the marriage ended and Justine Wilson wrote her side in her blog. She wrote about what happened during their marriage and how it ended.

The following events that happened had been a disaster for Musk. The public took Wilson's side on the issue of their marriage settlement. However, Musk's assets were hardly enough to give what Wilson wanted. Most of his properties were tied to SpaceX and Tesla Motors. They came up with another settlement to end the matter.

Bill Lee, one of Musk's closest friends, was worried about how these happenings can affect the **mental state** of his friend. He seemed to be close to having a *mental breakdown*. Lee went on a vacation with Musk to let him unwind.

Just some time after the divorce, Musk met the rising young actor, *Talulah Riley*, who played the role of Mary Bennet in Pride and Prejudice. Riley's father immediately made a background check on Musk after hearing about him from his daughter. Riley's father thought of his daughter as a fool for getting into a relationship with a divorcee with five children from previous marriages. Not heeding her father's advice, Riley agreed to married Musk without her parents' consent.

However, Musk's work didn't result in the same sweet ending. More problems sprouted in his **businesses** and **financial problems** became worse.

VantagePoint, as Musk believed, wanted to recapitalize *Tesla*. These future plans may not sound unreasonable but it was not the same goal that Musk had for Tesla.

SpaceX was not in a better situation. The lack of financial aid also resulted in more problems and challenges to the company that once held so much potential and promise. It was also rumored that they were losing the chance of taking the NASA contract. This contract can bring a huge amount of money to the company. However, something happened that changed all of these problems.

In **December 2008**, SpaceX was chosen to be the **supplier** for the ISS. The company received **$1.6 billion** to supply 12 flights to the space station. Musk's financial problems in SpaceX and Tesla Motors were solved.

Antonio Gracias, the founder of Valor Equity, saw how much Musk suffered and how he survived all of those downfalls. But he did more than just to survive. He continued to be focused on his job. Gracias respects Musk for his ability to take pain.

CHAPTER 9: LIFTOFF

Falcon 9, a rocket that launched from the Vandenberg Air Force Base, became the pillar of SpaceX. Musk was accustomed to launching a rocket; he's used to seeing how the flames occupy the rocket's base at liftoff, how the heavy object takes off to space, how it later becomes a tiny speck of light in the sky- Musk got used to all of these experiences.

SpaceX has constant operations. The company would send a rocket to space almost every month. These rockets contained *satellites* and *supplies* that it will then deliver to the ***International Space Station***. With this success, SpaceX became a well-known name in the aeronautics industry.

Unlike companies such as Boeing, Lockheed Martin, and Orbital Sciences, SpaceX does not rely on foreign suppliers. All of its materials are made in the **United States** and costs are cheaper. But despite the success of the space industry, many people do not know about its achievements. Companies sought the services of SpaceX to bring satellites to space and yet only a few people took notice.

Musk's line of thinking that the company should not rely on the government and limit their rocket launches every year enables the company to **push their limits** and make ***breakthroughs***. The boring side of the aeronautics industry became SpaceX's advantage.

People described Musk to be a **general** rather than a CEO. He recruits people that the SpaceX wants and lets them join his army. Having excellent grades and an excellent educational background may be important to work in SpaceX. But they give more focus on individuals with **type A personality traits**. They want to hire people who had been inventing and developing things since they were young.

Getting into SpaceX requires a lot of effort. Interviews and tests are common. The interviews can range from those **afternoon chats** to **mind breaking quizzes**. The answers to these questions are said to be rather complicated. Even though all the applicants undergo the thorough hiring process, engineers had more than just that. Applicants who passed these stages are asked to write a letter to Musk telling him why they want to work in SpaceX.

After completing all the challenges and tasks given to them, they will personally meet Musk for another interview. The interview can be one of two things. Musk would either ask the applicant several questions or just ask a big one. It was also expected for Musk to give the applicant riddles. But he is not interested if the applicant gets the answer right or not. He is more interested in the **way** the applicant **solves** the riddle.

The company has a high turnover. This is not unusual for companies in this industry. Nevertheless, Musk has something that can make a person believe in his ideals. Up to now, Musk is well respected by his current and even previous employees.

With the increase of capable employees and more hard work, SpaceX improved their launching capabilities. SpaceX could make developments, one after another, faster than any of its competitors could. One of the most important moment for the company happened when it launched *Falcon 9* with the **Dragon capsule** inside it. As the rocket boosted the capsule in space, Dragon was able to fly on its own. However, the struggle was just starting; the SpaceX crew had a hard time making sure that the capsule would safely dock in the space station.

NASA was quite pleased with the innovations of SpaceX and gave them **$440 million** to make improvements on the Dragon capsule. On May 2014, the world got its first look on the improved capsule named Dragon V2. The event was no ordinary exhibition. It seemed like a Hollywood kind of party. The public was amazed at what they saw inside Dragon V2. The inside of the capsule was spacious and rather stylish, unlike any space-bound vessels seen before. There was even a touch screen display like those seen in sci-fi movies.

However, Dragon V2 was just one of the projects that SpaceX had been working on. The company was working on what was to become the world's most powerful rocket – the Falcon.

With all the success of SpaceX, many employees believed that it was time to go public and have an *initial public offering*. The people working on this famous aeronautics company were generously paid but considering all the hard work and sacrifices that they gave for the company, they deserve more. Having an IPO will definitely have a huge effect on the wages of the employees.

However, Musk did not approve of the idea. With his experience with publicly listed companies, Musk knew better. Going public can greatly affect the **financial position** of the company. It may give them a profit but the *volatility* of the market can make or *break* the company. The employees will focus more on the *value of the stocks* rather than make **greater innovations**. Musk believes that SpaceX is not yet ready for an IPO. He might consider the idea but not now.

CHAPTER 10: THE REVENEGE OF THE ELECTRIC CAR

The innovations that the automotive industry had been so proud of did not really make much of a difference. The upgrades of these cars were *limited* to their **designs** and some **gasoline saving features**. Commercials and other forms of advertisements made it sound so amazing, but it was undeniable that the industry was sinking.

However, things changed in **2012** when Tesla Motors shipped the ***Model S sedan*** – a luxury car that is fully electric-powered and can travel **more than 300 miles** on just one charge. Unlike other luxury cars in the market, the Model S sedan can fit **seven people**.

The unique thing about Tesla's sales and marketing is how they do not sell their cars to dealer companies. Tesla has its **own stores** and **websites** that customers can visit to look at the offerings of this rookie in the industry.

Nevertheless, the success of Tesla came after a series of problems, company settlements, and malfunctions. Eberhard filed a lawsuit against Musk. He accused him of a couple of crimes and stated that he was not the true founder of Tesla. Musk is fully aware that he is not the true founder of Tesla and acknowledge the contributions of other people for its establishment. The fight between the two got worse. Past events were once again put into the spotlight.

Tesla became the subject of many news articles and reports but it was not because of its electric cars. The press flocked to see how the two co-founders would settle this feud. Eberhard and Musk decided to put an end to all these conflicts. Eberhard even **acknowledged the efforts** of Musk to push the company into more than what they once imagined.

People who could not get a grasp of Tesla's Model S sedan described the car as a fad. It did not receive the respect it deserved, and some people actually believed that such a development was *impossible*.

The company started from scratch in making the Model S sedan. In **2008**, Tesla's engineers bought a **CLS 4-Door Coupe**, which then became the basis for the style of Model S.

Franz von Holzhausen, a former intern at Ford and Volkswagen, was responsible for making the design of the sedan iconic. After graduating from college, von Holzhausen worked in Volkswagen for eight years. He became part of the team working on the new version of the Beetle. Von Holzhausen left Volkswagen and worked in the General Motors and Mazda as director of design.

Musk and his newly hired designer talked about the design of the car. Musk wanted the luxury car to accommodate seven people. It was a complicated idea, but von Holzhausen understood where his boss was coming from; Musk, after all, is a father of five. There was also the plan of having a **touch screen** installed in the car. Of course, there were times when two opposed the idea of the other. Nevertheless, after more brainstorming, they were able to conceptualize the design of the Model S sedan. The design of the car is an innovation that will change the public's view on automobiles. It will not be long before other companies in the industry will follow.

It was inevitable that the new car had issues; during the first few months, some Model S sedans suffered from malfunctions that were unreasonable for such an expensive car. Nevertheless, Tesla was able to fix these issues in a different manner. The way they solved a problem made it look like they were making **magic**.

The owner of the car did not need to go out of his house to get his car fixed. Overnight, a team of Tesla fixed the issues through the ***internet***. They downloaded **software updates** into the car to solve the problem. The next morning, the car works as if nothing ever happened the day before. The team also downloaded and installed other software updates in the car. The Model S sedan is a car that gets better over time.

Craig Venter, the man who decoded the human's DNA, described the car as a **computer on wheels**. Tesla turned into more than just a car with some awesome features. ***It became a gadget.***

Looking at the problems that Tesla experienced, it was remarkable on how successful it is now. It was such a disaster before. A lot of things were not functioning the way that they should.

Straubel said that the idea of electric cars had always been there but it was only ***Tesla*** who had the vision and the determination to actually make it. Musk's standards played a great role in the success of the company. They were able to make improvements that were not available in other ordinary luxury cars.

CHAPTER 11: THE UNIFIED FIELD THEORY OF ELON MUSK

With the success of Musk in his two companies, one might think that entering the aeronautics and automotive industries was enough. But Musk was nowhere done. He found another opportunity in another field: the **solar industry**.

The Rive brothers, Musk's cousins from South Africa, were also in the middle of achieving their own goals in life. They advertised their system just as how Kimbal went from one door to another to gather clients. What came after is the company made by Lyndon, Peter, and Russ Rive – the Everdream.

During a trip with Musk in **2004,** the bunch of adventurous fellas talked about what could be another challenge that they could take. While on the way to the camp, Musk told them about the opportunities in venturing into the **solar energy market**.

Musk, along with his cousins, were no experts when it comes to solar energy so they studied the industry for six months. During that time, it was not easy to have a solar panel. People were reluctant to invest on these products due to some *inefficiencies*.

Nevertheless, they started to put their ideas into action. The Rive brothers created **SolarCity** to make buying solar panels simpler and more efficient. The company didn't make their own panels. They buy everything and they install these panels on houses after making the necessary checkups.

SolarCity helps in making these panels more efficient. They even made a financing system that enables the consumer to **lease** the product instead of paying immediately.

Because of SolarCity, the electricity bill of consumers lowered. That's when Musk decided to help fund his cousin's company. He became the largest shareholder of SolarCity.

The company became the largest installer of solar panels in the country after six years. Their clients now include large corporations like **Intel** and **Wal-Mart**. SolarCity went **public** and its share price was high.

While SolarCity became a success, green technology companies located in Silicon Valley were suffering a downfall. Now, Elon Musk owns two of the most successful green technology companies in the country.

SolarCity's improvements were growing at a steady pace. The endeavors, as viewed by Musk, were essential for the future. But one of the most significant developments of the company was its acquisition of a **solar cell maker**. Through this, SolarCity does not have to purchase solar panels from other companies. They can finally make their very own.

Musk's companies worked together to produce better services and products to consumers. SolarCity began offering energy storage systems with the help of Tesla. With all the improvements of the company, SolarCity was inevitably a part of the utility industry. It became its goal to be the largest supplier of energy in the country.

SolarCity became the **unified theory of Musk** as his three companies helped each other. All the materials needed, manufacturing technologies, and factory operations were **shared**.

However, it was unavoidable that these companies became the subject of bullying by the other prominent establishments of the industries where they belong to. However, Musk knows better than to let this bullying get the best out of him.

What he is worried about is how his kids didn't experience enough challenges in their lives. Suffering helped Musk achieved what he has now. It made him strong but his kids cannot even imagine what he had been through.

Musk also considered the idea of having more kids. He said that it is the *responsibility* of smart people to procreate and pass on their knowledge to their children. He stated that countries with smart people, such as Japan and Russia, are suffering a low birth rate.

The future of Musk's companies is uncertain even if they are growing at a remarkable pace. However, he remains **optimistic** on the matter. He already laid plans on how these companies will continue.

Tesla plans on having five to six cars in its lineup as it becomes a renowned company in the electric car market. *SolarCity* has the potential of becoming a huge solar energy company. *SpaceX* has a more interesting future ahead with Musk's plans of having weekly flights. Its idea of sending humans and cargos to space through their capsules and landing with greater accuracy are just some of the developments they have in mind.

For over forty years of great hard work and a series of downfalls, Elon Musk is undeniably one of the best businessmen and innovators of his time.

Conclusion

The contributions of *Elon Musk* to the **aeronautics**, **automotive**, and **utility** industries paved way for more developments and a brighter future for mankind. He taught the world to push beyond the line known as a **boundary**.

Hold on to the dream that you had as a child and work hard to make it come true. This is a cliché taught from one child to another. But in Musk's case, he did not just work hard, he worked **insanely hard** to get to where he is now. The journey will be a **tough** one. A lot of people will discourage you. A couple more will **make fun** of you. But Musk's story will teach you that all of that is normal for a person who has a **goal in mind**.

Musk is a huge risk taker to the point that people calls him insane. His mind seems to work in the notion that success is all but a dream without risk. He had his own bad side. He was not entirely the hero that he admired on the video games he played as a child. But his story will surely inspire the world to get back on track after a failure. When Musk fell down, it was not part of his option to stop. He focused more and his mind wandered into how he could do better next time.

Looking back at all his experiences, one might find it hard to believe that he remained sane on those moments. His ability to move on immediately is definitely **awe-inspiring**.

His attitude of constantly wanting to make humanity's future a brighter one deserves more respect. It's not every day that the world sees a person as **dedicated** and **committed** as him. He is like one of those characters in movies who keep on saving other people even if it means risking their own lives. But what makes him different from these characters is that he does not risk his life into saving a city or a country from the bad guys. *He is willing to give up everything he has for the world as a whole.*

FREE BONUSES

<u>P.S. Is it okay if we overdeliver?</u>

Here at Readtrepreneur Publishing, we believe in overdelivering way beyond our reader's expectations. Is it okay if we overdeliver?

Here's the deal, we're going to give you an extremely condensed PDF summary of the book which you've just read and much more…

What's the catch? We need to trust you… You see, we want to overdeliver and in order for us to do that, we've to trust our reader to keep this bonus a secret to themselves? Why? Because we don't want people to be getting our exclusive PDF summaries even without buying our books itself. Unethical, right?

Ok. Are you ready?

Firstly, remember that your book is code: "**READ21**".

Next, visit this link: **http://bit.ly/exclusivepdfs**

Everything else will be self explanatory after you've visited: **http://bit.ly/exclusivepdfs**.

We hope you'll enjoy our free bonuses as much as we enjoyed preparing it for you!

CPSIA information can be obtained
at www.ICGtesting.com
Printed in the USA
BVHW070954010819
554877BV00001B/196/P

9 781646 151202